THE SILENCE

John Greening was brought up near Heathrow, and studied at Swansea, Mannheim and Exeter. Having worked for BBC Radio 3 under Hans Keller, he then joined Voluntary Service Overseas. He and his wife were sent to teach in Aswan, Upper Egypt for two years, and he was awarded the Alexandria Poetry Prize before publication of his earliest books, *Westerners* (Hippopotamus Press, 1982) and *The Tutankhamun Variations* (Bloodaxe, 1991). A dozen further collections followed, notably *Hunts: Poems 1979-2009* (Greenwich Exchange, 2009), and *To the War Poets* (Carcanet, 2013). Over the last decades, he has edited the work of Edmund Blunden and Geoffrey Grigson, produced several anthologies, and written studies of Elizabethan Love Poets, Yeats, Hardy, First World War Poets, Edward Thomas and Ted Hughes. Among other awards, he has won an Arvon (judged by Hughes and Heaney), the Bridport and a Cholmondeley. A long-time reviewer for the *TLS* and an Eric Gregory judge, he has appeared at the British Academy and Shakespeare's Globe, performing his own work or talking about other people's, and has contributed to various radio and television programmes. Collaborations include the sequence, *Heath*, with Penelope Shuttle, libretti for composers Cecilia McDowall and Philip Lancaster, and contributions to baritone Roderick Williams's Schubert Project. Since retiring from teaching, John Greening has held several Fellowships, most recently for the RLF at Newnham College, Cambridge.

Also by John Greening

Achill Island Tagebuch (Redfoxpress, 2019)
Ten Poems about Sheds (Candlestick, 2018)
Threading a Dream (Gatehouse, 2017)
Selected Poems of Geoffrey Grigson, ed. (Greenwich Exchange, 2017)
Heath, with Penelope Shuttle (Nine Arches, 2016)
Edmund Blunden's Undertones of War, ed. (Oxford, 2015)
Accompanied Voices: Poets on Composers (Boydell, 2015)
To the War Poets (Carcanet, 2013)

THE
SILENCE

JOHN GREENING

CARCANET

First published in Great Britain in 2019 by
Carcanet
Alliance House, 30 Cross Street
Manchester M2 7AQ
www.carcanet.co.uk

Text copyright © John Greening 2019

The right of John Greening to be identified as the author
of this work has been asserted in accordance with the Copyright,
Designs and Patents Act of 1988; all rights reserved.

A CIP catalogue record for this book is
available from the British Library.
ISBN 978 1 78410 747 5

Book design by Andrew Latimer
Printed in Great Britain by SRP Ltd, Exeter, Devon

The publisher acknowledges financial
assistance from Arts Council England.

Contents

Sibelius	7
On St Cecilia's Day	8
Nebamun's Tomb	9
Kew	16
Evensong	17
Bunker	19
1d	20
Heath	21
Rite	25
Woden	26
Chalk	28
Two Roads	33
X5	34
Stray Objects	35
Five Hilliard Miniatures	37
Fontevraud	42
Tree Rings	43
Unknotting	45
To a Lost Friend	48
Flight Path	49
Airmail for Chief Seattle	50
Totem	55
The Day	57
Visionary	59
Compleat	62

After Hölderlin: *To the Fates*	64
After Hölderlin: *Homecoming*	65
After Hölderlin: *Hyperion's Song of Destiny*	69
Under	70
From the Peak	71
The Silence	77
Notes	111
Acknowledgements	113

To my family

Silent, beyond silence listened for

SEAMUS HEANEY

THE SILENCE

Sibelius

It's January. A swan's wing overhead
reminds you of his Fifth
but also of his death, that skein
breaking away to circle him
as if to announce what year it was.

At this age, every instinct shouts
behind you – as it did at the panto
for the ghost – and there's an old man
at a lake still counting wild birds
who hasn't even noticed the time.

January is Janus's month. We should look
both ways. The geese have put their diversion
signs in the sky, but the sun holds up
its lollipop as if a young hero might
cross, find an egg, tie a knot in it.

2015

On St Cecilia's Day

Stop listening to that music
and hear instead
what the dead are saying
who were buried on this day
seven years or sixteen or,
if you insist on entering
the hypostyle court
to count the pillars,
a silent dynasty ago.

There is an absent
zodiac where the shifted
tropic once looked down
but one can imagine
the figures unless you
believe only in measurable
stars and cannot behold
even, say, the Southern
Cross with delight.

Now think of the day
a story that has been quietly
boring travellers to Syene
reaches north at last
through stacks and scrolls
to Eratosthenes, who sees
the sun-shaft in that well
and hears the Music of the
Earth start playing.

Nebamun's Tomb

I

Salt watches the saw cut a picture from his wall.
        The exquisite feathers fall from the lesser birds,
                tears of silt and straw from a hieroglyphic eye.

The Old Man sleeps in Great Russell Street and an image
        flashes. He is nowhere, somewhere on the West Bank
                or in the Underground. At Boughton House or buried

in a quarry near Corsham. The conservator
        lets the dancing girls go by, the wildfowl fly,
                balancing so carefully.

II

                enough to last you
      for eternity
             a thousand loaves
                        a thousand portions of flesh

a thousand different ornaments
                      changes
of clothing
        incense
              unguent
                      the saw stops
its noise
        and silence begins where that slot
ends above an owl who stares his meaning

full-face at us and goes on crying
across the food offerings, the desert pigments,
red and yellow ochre, frits of a ghostly blue

III

As in those dreams where you meet
equally with strangers and the dead you loved
that always seem to be set on a train
when they come to me, but here
follow the red lines of the tomb wall

to where the male guests are seated
like commuters from the afterlife
eating a wafer, holding a handkerchief,
one with a wig, some shaven-headed,
their lotus flowers *tssk-a-tssk*-ing

there are things you keep quiet about:
the double flute in the mouth of the girl
who looks straight at you, the entwined
haematite of the pair behind her,
the clap that has turned into a prayer.

IV

What lay in the mud between the lute on her breast
and the rack of nine pink stoppered wine jars?

A serving man unrendered as he reached for a drink?
So some scholars think, examining a muddy elbow.

But others are sure it is the last of the women, playing
an unknown instrument, one that is redolent of

wheat and barley, date fibre, reeds, rushes,
halfa, papyrus, tamarisk, fig or flax

together with some bones and fragmented flower heads.

V

Hard to imagine such a moment, naked girls
offering wine to both the men and to their wives,
part nightclub, part Academy Award Ceremony

where everyone has a fixed look on their face
until the prize is announced and there she goes
weeping into the lotus mic her thanks

to Henry for putting up the money, to Giovanni
for his skilful cutting and above all to…
but nobody is listening now, suppressing

their screams, they reach for the mandrake fruit.

VI

Some in baskets heaped as if they were stanza forms,
others massed into a flock of fifty syllables,
crammed like carvings on the Rosetta Stone,
the geese are here to be inspected.

The master sits in silence.
They too keep their beaks firmly shut.
Farmers can only prostrate themselves.

It is a scribe who finds something to say
as he opens a scroll before Nebamun
and begins to recite his poem: 'The Inspection
of the Birds at the Turning of the Year'.

VII

Get a move on! he shouts
as the cows pass by. It's like
watching paint dry. *And don't
talk, talking is what he hates!*

VIII

A fragment – why did this survive? – shows the barley
unharvested and upright with an old man bent over it
speaking to his own hand. As if an entire existence
had decomposed around him, yet he is fixed on this
augury in the lines of his palm. Over his shoulder
the grey mud-plaster encroaches like the North Sea towards
the cliffs at Dunwich. And above his earth-colour
a hieroglyphic armageddon hails on to his bald patch's
frizzy halo. Across the field from him the chariots
are ready to rumble off to war once the master returns,
who has leapt down to inspect the yields and convert them
into armaments. He has left his horse in the clutch
of a slave who can barely restrain its dark grey
from bolting out of the picture, having seen what's next.

IX

i bring you a hare
which i hold by the ears

it stares indignantly yet
knows it has the final

word   not only its fine
coat of yellow and white

with red speckling stripes
and black bristles   not only

its pink inner ears
and perfect whiskers   but that

the hare in hieroglyphics
means to exist

X

Let the empire spin
at the centre of this lunging
after birds that are so plentiful
nobody dreams of a time
when there is conservation. They fly
away into nothingness
to the swish of nets and stones
and guns and passages collapsing.
The fish too – mullet
and a fat puffer so pleased
with its poisonous self to be

on this white peninsula – sink.
A single butterfly is heading
for the hunter's toes and soon
African Queen, as it is known,
or Plain Tiger, will pass
into amnesia. Though there are
other humans, though there is
a goose that stretches optimistically
from the prow as the raised arm
swings against wagtail and wheatear
and shrike, it is the cat
carries the day, devouring
her soliloquy with a mouthful
of wing, her gold leaf eye
on the future, who will strike.

XI

There is a garden in the next world
where all the birds and fish and plants
that we have exterminated are being kept –

I think it is this seedbank that I visit
occasionally when I am sleeping and wake
to feel as if some part of me has gone out

and spent the night travelling, as Egyptians
used to believe and so would leave a false
door out of their tombs. Within that garden

which I imagine to be like the one at Kew
where my parents lived and where I was born
and taken through the penny turnstile

and in which there is no perspective, fish and ducks
lying sideways against the surface of the pool,
trees unfolded flat from its edges, yet where all

comes into a true angle because the light
is the light that was in Egypt when we were there,
the fragmentation of the tomb will hardly matter.

This will be enough: just as a speck of DNA
can reconstruct the scene, the life, I am hoping
that in this garden there is somewhere that I can learn

to plant and grow things as I never let myself
be taught by my father or to pave a proper path
as I watched my mother do. There will be fruits there –

I can see them in this last surviving scene, the dates,
the figs, the ghastly dom. But also grapes. And some papyrus
for writing on too, if in that garden writing is allowed.

Kew

To Occupation Road again,
a whole year nearer my own
retirement now. The track slopes
down past the Record Office
to the river. I am looking for
any of the soft fruit canes

my grandfather planted, but find
instead a stag beetle upside
down on the tarmac, struggling
like a memory, the feelers at full stretch.
Maybugs! she shudders. The pathway
ends at the Thames, where I note

flood defences, vaguely recall
the waterworks, and suddenly they
have found me as a train breaks
through the overgrown embankment.
I want to look up and see my father
at the glass, returning, and wave to him.

Evensong

in memory of Dennis O'Driscoll

How strange to have lost those close to us. It's not possible
that so much can be extinguished. I think of the daguerreotypes
Victorians had taken with their dead propped next to them
in an armchair or stretched on a couch. That's how it feels.

And more believable than that everything just ends is what I've read
in samizdat, or off a high shelf ('The Occult') – that the afterlife
is much like this one, that we carry on, having created
already our heaven or hell. First, though, the 'halls of healing'

where we sort out griefs and grudges. A comforting thought? Evidently
not, since people won't even think about it. And particularly
in church, where no priest dare bring up the one thing
we really want to know – what happens when we die?

Of course, to find when it ends that life goes on would likely
come as a shock to many who had depended on annihilation.
Suddenly there's no escape. Not judgment as such
but the curtain rising on a scene you thought was over, rather

like those opera productions that they go on reviving through
the decades. A man loves two women. A woman
leaves Francesco for Dante. But the protagonists keep singing,
the invisible orchestra playing its heart out in the pit.

And where is the impresario behind all this? Too eagerly
we've bundled Him off to some old props room labelled 'Heaven'
with clouds, haloes, the key, a whole iconography; though angels –
angels such as Blake would talk to… I hear a voice

remarking dryly that our angels are the Celtic Twilight's fairies.
Which stage have you reached now, my friend? Your life's work
was facing up to death (having lost your parents young)
and duties. You died this Christmas Eve. And where is God?

That may not be the question. Why bring the Deity
into a process that might be going on quite happily without Him?
It's not *Gerontius*. And there are still so many drop-scenes
between 'departing soul' and 'the presence of the Almighty'.

None of which is something you'd want to bring up
at dinner parties. If a Nobel Prize-winning poet
can still be mocked for such beliefs, no chance for me.
Instead, I mutter my speculations to the cat who sits here

purring at my right hand, warm in this wooden box
where I have spent it seems an eternity holding a pencil,
reading, listening to 'Complete Works' and vicariously visiting
the rest of the world through liquid crystal. If I died

right now, it's possible I wouldn't even notice, except
some difference in the atmosphere, the way I could move, more like
a dream-drifting; and there would be people I didn't recognise
all in the same boat; and somehow the pressure of urgency

as if there were an unspoken mission... No wonder they scoff:
you could power half Cambridge with the laughter in the wind
tunnel where they test the latest versions of the engines
that drive their clockwork. A medieval bell strikes.

Too long since anybody could speak about such matters, at least
here in the West. 'The rest is silence' is our watchword
and 'Ay, but... to go we know not where'. I think we know
more than we think. Well, well, 'we shall find out'.

Bunker

A space of pouring
darkness, the rush
of a time crushed

to small black
lumps of smokeless
childhood. There goes

the leathern back
of the man with
an empty sack.

Id

Britannia, I can smell the sweat of your copper mines
even as you loll there waiting for the diamond jubilee's
automata to run down. Look at you,

almost lost against the blackened walls of a ONE
PENNY world. Your shield would not keep out
a Boer let alone resist that Prussian advance.

Your trident thrusts up into the thumb and fingers
of a Victorian on the Clapham omnibus, oblivious
to the threat of a retaliatory strike. The Romans

in twelves and twenties from the direction of the Mint
stamp out the flicker of anything that looks like change.
Yet you are already weary of the endless arcadia

and yearly the other side of you grows blanker, less amused.

Heath

for Penelope Shuttle

I

This is a dry, dangerous place, away from the river,
from the everyday, its safe demands. The last mill's wave,

a hovel's distant wink. With a drink (*to change!*), their talk
rattling like chainmail, a pair go riding under the gibbet

and into the dark, all battles behind them. The Bath Road
or the Staines Road? Neither can avoid that bleak exposure

where the enlisted will be drilled, where invading forces muster,
without one church spire to contradict the horizontal,

a zone you enter to find yourself heading towards yourself,
free of the march, the taut spring, into a timelessness,

a fencelessness. Our famous Heath. Its enormous absence
of anything but lizard, buzzard, kite and mouse,

no coppice or hedge or field, but an unenclosed pack
of wildtracks, furze, bog; then a single roding nightbird

and a final call for the wolf of Perry Oaks. You are far
from the Bell Inn, the comforting tree-song of the High Street's

untongued as they swing, grow greener by the month,
or feel the warp of a ribcage shot by a fresh south-westerly.

II

Stop. Listen. Nothing but the invisible drone in the air
of *bombus terrestris* taking off from the heather, at work
while others sing.
                        But the songsters have all gone away for August,
leaving the cricket, the clockworking alarm of game birds,
and a stonechat to chip at time.
                              I am humming
through familiar numbers, all beginning on G,
descending to a ground bass. Broom. Bracken. Broom.
Tormentil.
               It is good to step in to the open, unknown,
not wearing a mask, not needing to, alive in the sun
and with no intention of holding anyone up.
                                     The mail
is allowed to pass by, its horses panting. We came
looking for quiet.
                   If I had taken a deer, and seen
my eyes put out by the Conqueror's men to pay for it,
all I would know now is the nightjar and some white noise
from a pair of doves who are longing for one single tree.

Uneasily, one senses something overhead, that hovers –
an envoi from the powers that be, spying, naturally, on low-
life here without licence.
                         'Poaching?'
                                    'Hunting, your Honour,
a quiet day, or days.'
                      A dangerous cloud, the colour
of money, scuds a missel thrush towards us, followed by
flashes – thousands of them, from some peninsula of connectedness
and constantly crashing waves – crying their fame, and mewing
crazèd ideas, a thousand drafts of the unlistening future.

III

It is night now on the great track, among the weirs
and warrens
            not even the moon has control here
                                      guidance
must be what the eye can snatch from obscurity, catching either

huge iron wheels that will plunge you to Bath by dray,
by draft, gouging the mind to clods and furrows, conquest,

or the quiet light hooves of whatever was hired in Hounslow
clever enough to nip
                across country
                            at the first click
of flintlock
        muzzled
                flash in the pan
                            and hellfire curse.

Of course, for those who are not afraid of witches, there is
this weird crossing to be made on foot, if we are lucky

avoiding the upturned waggon, its cold, silent passengers,
that fleet steed from the Bell stuck fast and sinking.

And there is always the ghost of the long lost, long
straight Roman road, its agger obscured by heaps
of baggage, pannage, sewage, droppings on New Age
sheeptracks that trace a zodiac or a maze round a distant tor…

In truth, the Heath can only be negotiated with closed eyes

by letting what's out there start up its ghostly scan

by enduring interrogations from ice and filth and law

by passing through the gate of clay or the gate of gravel

Rite

a high bassoon, it stretches

        its long neck like the first

                goose in a v

                        that knows

                                spring

                        is here

                but there is one

        last battle to be fought

with ice, with air, white-fronted

Woden

Masked and mounted
on an F-15
from Lakenheath,
he is cutting edge

circling again
and now again
Grime's Graves
where the spear began

its flight towards
flintlock, towards
no-man's-land
and moonscape.

How to clear
the forest and all
its fears? Dig
pits with seven

antler picks
to the flickering of
a chalk lamp
in the shadows

with a phallus
and a white goddess
heaving to give
birth to blackness.

Flint will carve
an opening along
the Icknield Way
and split the carcass

of Europe into skin
and guts and meat
and bones. What remains
will be what he owns

and is beneath him
as he spins thunder
from the cocoon
of his own silence.

Chalk

To walk on the horse's eye was the aim –
the same eye that has watched you growing up
since you rolled under it, turning and turning
green while the shape around it has been scoured
by holystones. Still the White Horse appears
above the blackthorn on the road to Frome,
flash of vitrescence, vision that endures
the cement works beneath it whose plume blurs
and feathers across borders. Just to see
would be enough, as time's optometrist
props up a sign and asks: better or worse?

*

    Clay is the place
    where I put my foot down
    but chalk I live by
    and ride its imaginings.

*

    For example, the workshop
    where I'd handed round some lines
    about Uffington and as
    synchronicity or luck
    would have it the same image
    was suddenly hanging there
    on a silver chain (that was
    yours, poet). Since when, other
    mysteries than whether it's
    horse, dragon or sky-spider

have shuttled through, though not to
the Ridgeway's march-time, rather
from somewhere higher, hidden,
where minds draw on each other.

*

As you come in, look:
a blackboard cast out from
Port Sunlight, ghosts of words
left as she left.

*

A kind of stability is what I remember
about my childhood. So if we had a long weekend
we would all go for a long walk to see the Long Man
of Wilmington, admired by my father, the stickler
for all that was upright and proper and my mother
was happy to follow its broad gauge tramlines to where
ever they led... All dissolved in half a century's
downland rain, yet there he is now rising once again,
the Lone Man, the Green Man, the acceptable faceless
face of mystery in the otherwise clear-glazed, *Snow-
cem*'d, trim and clockwork lives Middlesex levelled us to.

*

To a past which had water,
limestone, granite, gold,
but no chalk, we took our
present of dust.

*

These days, only when there's a party
of students do I see Cerne Abbas
and then it's a minibus, no time
to climb the hill let alone pursue
fertility rites or anything
further than the glass wall where Hardy's
study has been relocated, yet
this is an icon of unabashed
Englishness, up for a laugh, to hell
with propriety, defying mere
reflection, books, words, though pointing at
what's underneath it all: the same chalk
that song-walled Hitler, the same broad grin
and outrageous flash of English teeth.

*

    Pick up the cue, apply
    the small red cube:
    take aim, and
    split the prism to a pack of eyes.

*

The pattern no one else can see, the one found
by sounding with an iron bar so that piece
by piece a picture chalks itself on the brain.
This, after all, is an individual
who believes in the power of the pendulum,
in dowsing, who expects us to accept this
wild speculation. Cambridge keeps its distance,
each college bell striking out the correct hour
and leaving the undertones to the under-
graduates who probably came up with this
pair of giants (Gog, Magog) in the first place.

*

      Hopscotch your way home
      counting the steps down into
      that cul-de-sac
      you set off to school from.

*

Where the Icknield Way crosses Ermine Street, where the ley lines meet
outside Ladbrokes, there is a grating in the pavement that kids
can drop gum down or worse. It is the original cave mouth
though not a cave, more a well, womb or subterranean hive
crawling with lines that turn into limbs and then take on features
that start to tell tall stories seven metres or more below
the high street, a temple hacked into a bell shape that summons
Knights Templar out of hiding from its thirteenth-century walls.
St Christopher is dancing with the Christ Child on his shoulder.
Katherine clutches the wheel while Michael demonstrates his sword.
The hand of God has released a dove towards the bookmaker's.
But who would have bet on these tumbling horses, these fallen knights
or on this roistering sheila who throws up her skirt and thrusts
so hard at the entrance that the cocky eyes of youth are shrunk
to a bunch of violets? All done in chalk, says the teacher,
in bas relief, though covered with graffiti and flickering
today to the flash of iPhones as the local history
society's cassette player drones on about James the First,
who when he came here might have… We leave this wonder up the slope
of a passageway that could be in the Valley of the Kings
but which takes us back out into the sunlight of Hertfordshire
and Royston, its pedestrian crossing, its charity shops.

*

On the South Downs or the North
pick this micro-
chip of fossils up: sea
life is what you see.

*

My mother's origins are lost, they crumble
away at Folkestone; on my father's side
the graves remain in Deal, near Caesar's landing,
unwritten lives that might as well have been
in Roman Britain for all we know of them
or of the hand they had to gamble with
before the chips were finally swept away
to leave a green baize and the waves unfolding,
folding, overcoming the chalk. Though chalk
that crumbles also filters. And can write.

Two Roads

There are the fast people
who check their emails hourly,
engage with Twitter and multi-
task their way through the day.

And there are the slow ones
who never reply even to your third
request, and almost miss
meetings and prefer pencil.

The first – the fast – will be
up to advise the worm,
to value the cup, to out-tweet
all competitors, whatever.

The last (the least hurried),
nevertheless, and surprisingly
it has to be said, will,
as in fact it turns out,

succeed just as well,
catching what the others
were moving so quickly they missed:
the prize deep-feeders.

X5

The bus slows at the dancing
blue and ignis fatuus
of yellow vest and chequered
bodywork. There's one car
in the ditch and one with an L
slewed across the featureless
straight run from Cambridge.

Our driver rolls down
the glass – *five or six hours,
it's as bad as it gets* – and lets
the swish and flip and grim
theatricality as emergency
vehicles keep arriving
(cutting tools, the doors

of an ambulance swung back)
enter the overheated bus
alongside cold rumour.
Caxton Gibbet watches.
So do the chicken bones
of that restaurant we had booked
for the day of the fire. Blinded

by oncoming might-have-beens
and unscripted write-offs,
we are redirected out
of the terrifying limelight
backstage towards Papworth,
hoping there's a way through
Yelling perhaps or Graveley.

Stray Objects

They roll about our time-picked skulls.
They split us into particles like skittles.
They rock Newton's cradle where we lie.

Quartz. Flint. Slate. Chalk.

They carry us with them in our pockets.
They give you something touching to remember.
They lead silently through the sinking ways.

Heart. Egg. Eye. Gall.

Polished apotheoses of tor and sill
and spit and banked storm beach, they each
offer their cure for our chronic stammering.

*

    to take our transparency
    and draw it out

    of the bolt that welded
    the desert sand

    into a vessel for flowers
    or for the lips

    or with a breath into
    blue hollow-ware

                        or in a square
                        reflect on the passing

                        hub running its lodes
                        out of silica fen

                                    *

While the bus   turns at the crossroads   grumbling and smoking
the secrets hum to themselves inside their inviolable nucleus
While the age   flashes by   for the sake of a picture
the orbiting of object around its beauty knows no terminus

                                        Kettle's Yard, Cambridge

Five Hilliard Miniatures

I

The ground
zeros in on
her knowing smile:
lofty, distant, trying to say
there may well be renascent grey
but this brow intends to keep it off, chin
held sharply up and hatched into those wry
flesh pink tones reserved for quiet subjects.
Oh, she can laugh the high boots off a cavalier,
but dignity and poise prevail; some well
chosen, well placed jewels at neck, ears and breast
from India, from Ethiopia,
a hand just out of sight, feeding
a favourite pet. This could be
our queen, were it
not for the stars,
the stripes.

II

A ground
of carnation
as convention
requires, but the features pale, eyes
cast down. Her clothes are not those of
royalty, rather she is dressed for day
to day, plain blue, hair up, no ornament,
a sieve dangling from her hand. Yet she knows
the Field of Cloth of Gold was in her own lifetime.
Her eyes are on her book. Behind her swept
back chestnut hair some silver lines appear
in fine calligraphy and spell her name,
the artist's name. We feel that strains
of a lute must be playing as
she sits for him
some touch, some grain
of love.

III

No ground
is visible –
there is so much
elaborate allegory,
emblem and 'imprese'. He is shown
full length, leaning against a tree: scattered
armour, two ravens, a pansy, a shield
with motto (green, engraved) – and even a
memento mori, which pops out when you stand at
a certain angle. A skull. One can't help
feeling the artist is having a joke
behind our age's brand-named back: *Look – I'm
unique!* He has the cheek also
to put himself into his own
work of art for
cognoscenti
to spot.

IV

Grounds for
complaint: why have
you made me look
so surly? Elizabeth would
have had the artist's lead chopped off.
But that's the point, ma'am. You will notice that
he has stained you subtle, witty, wildly
intelligent. This was commissioned by
a Fellow of New College. It has been handed
down to us and is the one true likeness
gazing to vanishing point without airs,
with sure perspective. If the graphite blurs
it's because this was the only
sitting, caught with friends, with her flute
in hand as the
tilt began for
favours.

V

What ground
lies under this
exquisitely
limned rendition, these features so
intent on how ten fingers can
make their quaintest interlacing of line
with line, of melody with word, at time's
virginals? It is the same carnation
on a playing card that's under every face here.
From this one rose these bice and crimson stems,
this intricately blossoming lace ruff,
lawn veil or stippled silver coronet,
though always (as the Cast Shadow
Master insists) throwing a dark
confessional
patch on the wall
behind.

Fontevraud

Out of a forest more
silent than strictest vows,
through walls that once
confined a royal line,

to see Eleanor, with
Henry, Richard, and John's
queen, lying on stone,
untroubled by a twitter

of nesting from the cloisters
that raise serene white
eyebrows at something still
keen to escape the knot

of box hedging. Noon.
The world sends its chimes.
The abbey reaches out
to recover its lost hours.

Tree Rings

for Katie at 30

Before the Reverend Goodchild cut them down,
you used to like to hide behind those trees
that outgrew themselves: leylandii.

There were two knotholes in the larch-lap
where a setting sun would make at a certain point
a kind of devil's gaze. It was a place

to play away the years. And there were others,
some of which we only guessed about,
school clearings, river crossings, or away

in an ice maze or a scheherazade of sand,
where the same tree grew uncontrollably
and the same grim eyes stared through.

*

Sequoia in the distance; horse chestnut candles between;
and close by, the ash, with rose tangled in it.

No bad prospect for a child. You used to hear
doves (and occasionally mice) scratching the flat roof.

There were other noises too, inexplicable ones.
And there below your window, the old woman's well.

*

At the bottom of the garden where now a paperbark maple uncurls,
discarding another draft, there are the remains of that black poplar,

the one I proudly tracked down and planted, not the hybrid
street tree from Manchester, but our native *betulifolia*,

of which there are fewer than ten thousand left, or so I believed
when it grew into your favourite hanging-out place. The swing I had
    rigged

from one of its three massive stems became for a single summer
a glade, a sacred grove to cradle you and your book, until

one night in a millennial wind the whole thing torquing
to itself, groaned, then collapsed across the fence, almost as far as

our neighbour's greenhouse. The swing was crushed. I am to this day
angry, and thankful, and astonished that such a bough could ever have
    held you.

Unknotting

Hawthornden, 2010

BUZZARD

    rests briefly on the ash
    that's just putting out leaves

    makes no sound among the chaffinches
    and blackbirds and reiterated note

    from the rubbish vans in the outside
    estate. He is doing his rounds

    looking for garbage to collect
    wheeling among the crows

    that are scattered like bin bags.

CLEARING

    holly and yew
    and rhododendron

    do not like
    the light

    manners and
    flippant quips

of the larch
and birch

we do not welcome
your double

meanings
they say, leaving

the oak to lean
towards his dark

singular justice
without a wise

crack and with his
hanging cap on

DISPLAY

    Beech going off like the most expensive
firework in the forest, exploding
into light green light that lights

the dim ravine and says books
like mine are not only leaf-turners
but on the Hawthornden longlist.

PRAISE FOR

Too many poets have been here.
They cry on all sides
read us, read us.

Birches are faded spines
embossed with lichen
or illegible as Morse.

Insects quote their way up
to a drop of blurb.
The wrappers peel.

And at our feet, new clover
and bedstraw and nettles,
all the fiddleheads.

I'll be that log the moss
is engrossed in, invisible
except for one knot.

To a Lost Friend

You look at me with vague recognition as someone might stand
before a Rothko at the Tate. The turbines have long been removed
but the outside's quite unchanged since I first saw your watercolour
wolds and lowland pastels, with figures from the French court
on swings, or playing a ball game, and children running happily
hither and yon, as you look on, with a shrug or a wink:
you knew the dewpond where they dumped all the Chippendale,
you knew where the moat was, the priest-hole. But names…

Now the fingerposts and milestones have been removed, as if
preparing for some war, they will not come. Why should you
recall this warm face through your mist? Even the hospitals
at Hillingdon, at West Middlesex, cover up what happened,
their car parks blacking out everything except
precise arrival times; and we will be charged.
I want to mention Hobbema or a seascape high on a wall
in a stately home that shows a tall ship sinking.

But such corridor conversations have gone down
in a wreck of gilt frames, appendices, smashed archives
to where even that allegory you explained to me of Saturn
devouring his own children is lost on the blank horizon
of a minimalism your old art can only smile at.
You smile, and I think of green paint wet still
on your set for a one-man open air performance:
the lights go up for the opening lines, but no one enters.

Hounslow Heath

Flight Path

The plane carrying Geography passes over towards Heathrow
    and it says *The map I am following is signed Speed*

The plane carrying History passes over towards Heathrow
    and it says *Here is the paper. I have folded it into a dart.*

The plane carrying Chemistry passes over towards Heathrow
    and it says *My cauldron! My crucible! My melting pot!*

The plane carrying Physics passes over towards Heathrow
    and it says *Boom!* but only after it has vanished

The plane carrying Biology passes over towards Heathrow
    and it says *Fly Pandemic. Jet Lag. DVT.*

The plane carrying Maths passes over towards Heathrow
    and it says *Given that you have real roots, go figure*

The plane carrying Art passes over towards Heathrow
    and it says as it brushes Green Belt with its shadow

'The plane carrying Design passes over towards Heathrow
    and has a better idea'

The plane carrying Religious Studies passes over towards
    Heathrow (spire, minaret) looking for crop circles

The plane carrying French, Spanish, German, Chinese, Gujarati,
passes over towards Heathrow and says nothing

The plane carrying English passes over towards Heathrow
    and keeps on going

Airmail for Chief Seattle

Let him be just and deal kindly with my people,
for the dead are not powerless. Dead, did I say?
There is no death, only a change of worlds.

Recalling how in our English hurry
to 'stand in line', to go and bury
American hatchets, we took that ferry
in '99 out to the island,
your burial place, I fall silent
and shuffle towards the check-in salient.

Sixteen years. Before the cancer's
white cellular advance
across our bloodline and its chances.
Before the towers, the fall, the raven
repeating *more*. A kind of heaven.
What world, Seattle, do you live in?

That day I had the one mission
and one bus to the reservation
to show our children your lost nation.
Instead, I think they rather lost me.
Your words confronting death possessed me.
Death. I cannot put it past me.

And meanwhile, we have to live it.
We carry on and try to laugh it
off – *a 'change of worlds'? I love it!*
If only you had perhaps expanded,
we could approach the scan unhounded
by fears: what if all this ended?

It's time to tap into your knowing
cloud again. We've finished queuing.
Security's through. We'll soon be flying,
baggage free: the tunnels beckon,
the door, the smile, the seat not taken,
a smooth ascent, this sudden sicken-

ing plunge: an air canoe, shooting
rapids, in slow motion, fighting
nothingness, passengers courting
hollywood, i-power, the electronic
tundra, and stifling oceanic
yawns of fear. Don't panic.

It's time for me to write this letter.
On either side a grown-up daughter
and here, their mother. The pitter-patter
of tiny keys as I carve a totem
posting. Should I start at the bottom
or aim high? Dear Atom-

Splitter-in-Chief, forgive me prying,
but do you not remember saying
that when our children's children are playing
and think themselves alone, the shadow
spirits will come to them, that the dead are…
What precisely was your credo?

A child of Hounslow Heath, I conjured
paleface friends to get an injun
scalping in our garden, urged on
by Pan Am drumrolls, feathers, war paint,
'let's pretend'. Even Dick Turpin's
night flight was impotent

to hold us up, our timeless, rootless
idea of prairie: to fly footloose
from suburbs, ululating outlaws.
And yet it's not as if your people
were on our radar. The Bramley apple
above my head was home. That couple's

wigwam of runner beans. The tribal
elders of my sacred land who kindle
a bonfire, beat a cake, dwindle
to nothing below me as we leave the heathen
childhood backways, leaping our hawthorn
hedge, the mayflower; and find another

kind of world. Is this your answer?
Icefields, smoke, a glacier, a geyser,
a change of flights where people dance
away the darkless nights all summer
and keep the ghosts for winter, the murmur
of *huldufolk,* Odin, a rumour

of Spirit Guides. I came, following
my father's death, looking for Valhall,
a camp where he spent his war trawling
the ether for U-boats, and didn't
talk, but sensed perhaps the hidden
explosive depths. He would have trodden

respectfully the razor lava
you could walk with ease, lover
of the claw, the red tooth, believer
in magic. Is it this you inhabit
when not steaming through the carpet
at Microsoft or Boeing? The cockpit

has a new voice: we're cruising
etc... but what I'm raising
goes higher still. People are dozing.
So shift those plates and let your shaman
secrets flow, play me
that change of worlds. Or will it scare me

as much as this weird passage over
Greenland, Baffin Bay, a cove
or lake, waste that goes on for ever?
I'm ready to make the right connections,
to say that it's like when that white taxi
brought my friend to the funeral, tricksily

stepping from an ad for Icelandair
as a short-circuit in my mother's wiring
caused her doorbell to start *whirring...*
And no answer on Bainbridge Island
that day we came to you from England
to visit what had been your own land,

'a place of clear still water' stretching
below us now. We change direction.
Unplug my ears. There, crouched
on grass beside your grave (a dreamwork
of dug-out timbers, a mythic framework)
we saw SEALTH, and headed homewards.

Sixteen years since then. Our girls are
savvy smartphone users (the wheels
go down), their past a fading pulsar
full of messages. A sense of falling
back and forwards. Silently calling
(an ancient device), I catch a smiling

face in the cloud, a wrinkled mountain,
wink from a lake, a shadow hunting
over forest and freeway now haunting
its own grounded self, but nothing
from your side. The door, scything,
releases us, our breathing.

Totem

Cedar man says
come out of that
old chest and start
climbing again
Halibut man
says catch the sea
and let it lift
you from flatness
Double-headed
snake says to the
doubts listen and
they say listen
Whale says there she
blows there above
the round tower's
far escape wheel
Raven says but
memory knows
something that is
going to fall
Sea otter says
then it's time to
do nothing but
play in the waves
Thunderbird says
conquerors fight
their way to the
top of the pole
Old man says but
my view of the
polo club is

quite adequate
Bear says I am
above you all
you barefaced low-
down losers look
The Man with a
large hat, barely
audible, says
actually no

Virginia Water

The Day

The day the sky began to fill with skeins of silver dots
was the day #Columbus started trending. For a few weeks

we lived beneath this Fabergé food cover, it became
the fabric of our lives, the way we once let Kodachrome

roll over in the face of all those pixels, and forswore
our books of happy holiday prints. Did the UN speak?

Did anyone send up a missile? We would never know,
and no one reported it. The chat shows went on chatting,

the news remained securely in orbit, obsessed by it,
but impotent; until one morning the flat screens simply

turned round and there it was, more extraordinary than
anyone in the movies had ever imagined, yet

after so many shots in the dark, we were able to
synthesise all such attempts into helping us conceive

what we were meant to see – and though it wasn't Ridley Scott
or Spielberg, something familiar seeped into that blue light.

If there was a face, it didn't have eyes or ears or nose.
If there was a voice, it rose and fell as a kind of song.

But any doubts that from this day on we would be classed as
the heathen, that here now was the latter-day Word of God,

were quickly dispelled. We were shown precisely what to do.
Instructions were the kind you see on the side of a box

exhorting you to employ correct lifting procedures.
By sunrise we were on our way, carrying what we must,

some water, our children, the suggested selection of
music and books, no luxuries, nothing old world, and those

who couldn't… they felt there might be another way. We left
food in the fridge, hanging baskets, a security light.

Visionary

I

It seems I have stirred up dream-envy
on Facebook (with some flattery – 'a real
poet's dream') though it fades, my Friends,

as quickly as delight at having touched
the real that comes so rarely, but sets
the whole apple tree ablaze with coincidence

and connection. I dreamed of Samuel Palmer,
spoke to him, read lines with him,
passed comment on the work of Young –

and, yes, we'll interpret that as Jung,
just as my Sam was partly a character
from *The West Wing*, though in the dark,

high-collared coat of the period
he felt to me like one of the Ancients.
'What did you talk about?' the community

wants to know. But even the faces
have gone. Words went as I switched
the darkness on and knew what I liked.

II

I wanted to show you our elm, Sam, the last one remaining
at the end of the lane. It hangs on, a true English Elm,
not like this Japanese imitation I planted where the car is parked

that came (an offer in *The Listener*) through the letterbox and now threatens
our internet connection. It marks the beginning of the open field
out where the dog barks at Banks's Farm, the only light

from a tower, red, fixed, not Milton's Platonist, I'm afraid,
but Little Staughton's airfield, where businessmen jet in and out,
though last night there were sky lanterns for the New Year drifting

unblinking as a line of apprentice angels. I'd like to have heard you tell me
about the day the moon rose behind your elm and cast shadows
and Mary Ward repeated those lines from the poet Young – *the vision*

of a moment made, dream of a dream, and shadow of a shade – a moment
that set burning and aloft the life of Palmer. I could have pointed out
the house where the Blakes live, descendants of your friend, with a pool, dogs,

original features. You would have mimicked him and then transfigured
this shepherdless age, found shadows, though the trees that cast them once
have gone to disease, found moonlight, though our new red calendar

shows only a single solitary black circle for this day:
a desert place we have flown to, set down on, walked over,
yet failed even to begin to know as you did with your eagle vision.

III

I pick through countless scattered frames and lenses,
the dust and verdigris, the scratchings of a lifetime,
bifocals past, varifocals unprofitable,
the buy-one-pair-and-get-another-pair-free drawer,
to these silver spectacles of Samuel Palmer.

From printed pages of my woodbound fastness
I look out towards the bottom of the garden:
the gap in the hawthorn is a gold-leaf halo,
and that bright figure, that crimson figure waiting
to climb the silver birch as it glows, is it her?

No, she's gone south, far south, where holy palmers
learn to kiss. It's just a pheasant and what turns it
red in the hedge now is not May or even Elder,
but sunset through the gap I made for emergency
delivery of a sofa, for watching television.

Compleat

To set off on my bike at first light,
pass through the gates and down the avenue
of horse chestnuts towards Robert Adam's
creation, the low roar of the M4 ahead,
and of the Great West Road

and take from its light brown nylon sleeve
the varnished split-cane lengths of my rod
and fit them together, attach the multiplying
reel with its fine line of a breaking strain
I can't now recall,

fasten the hook, using a knot, however,
I can remember (around three times
and back through the loop), adding the float,
a simple quill like the kind of pen Dickens
or even Shakespeare used,

scattering groundbait, before kneeling
to open a tin of maggots like the contents
of a skull, its imagery, stick one on the barbed
point of the hook, or pierce the flesh of a lugworm
dug from a sea mist,

so to cast, to feel the free line
sizzle across the surface and its speed ravel
off the unclamped reel: then to sit
on the edge of the lake at Osterley Park
quite lost in watching,

was a joy, an intensity of youthful delight
no poet could capture, though I only ever
caught roach, some minnows, not the long desired
bottom-feeding tench, nor the tremendous
episcopal rainbow.

After Hölderlin: To the Fates

An die Parzen

Give me just one summer, you powers that be,
    plus an autumn for more mature utterance
        so this 'I' can leave, feeling keen to,
            and satisfied by a sweet rendition.

The soul that missed out on its god-given right
    in this life will not find much rest in the next.
        Yet if I could achieve that holy
            grail of my wholeness, the perfect poem,

I'd go willingly into silence obscure
    and be content there, even if I can't bring
        my singing skill along with me: once
            I had godly powers – that will have to do.

After Hölderlin: Homecoming – To My Family

Heimkunft – An die Verwandten

I

Out on the Heath, night still glows as approaching images
   shine in the pleasure of travel and skim the pre-war semis.
From Staines to Bell Corner, screeching broomsticks blast
   above rowan, birch and maidenhair with a sly wink.
Slowly the rush hour struggles around its eagerness to get away –
   children or hardened travellers, all squabbling affectionately
between hotel and multistorey: it accelerates, brakes,
   speeds off again to the drunkenness of imminent escape.
There, a year is nothing but endless holidays, a shuffling
   sleight of lands on the pilgrim arrivals and departures board.
The Bird of Thunder, meanwhile, stacked high and circling,
   knows all destinations and announces that day is about to break.
Below, curtains are pulled back on bedroom windows
   and from duvets each cold eye meets this high processional.
They know expansion is inevitable; they have heard the groaning by night
   (as others before heard Druids), the reversing engines howl,
spilling kerosene, ruining maths lessons, music recitals.
   The engineers never cease, night or day. It is a gift.

II

Peacefully glittering, the silver tubes pass over
   the clouds, rose-tinted above their Himalayan snowline,
and higher still beyond the stratosphere, the unblinking orbits
   of the future trace their plans, the shuttles, stations, satellites
and whatever unspoken possibilities the Deus ex Machina decides

as it looks down clairvoyant on the cloud the age has created
for its pleasure, for its pastimes: enough wire to entangle ourselves
   but not to hang with these highwaymen at the Bell where new
                                               developments –
the mall and leisure centre and luxury apartments – proclaim
   green shoots for the drought-afflicted, an ozone summer,
the cumulus humilis drifting, the windsock proud.
   Even that slow cortege towards the crematorium seems
off on the journey of a lifetime as, passing the demolished Regal,
   you recall *The Sound of Music* or where Memorydiscs began
your first *Unfinished* and something touches the very depths, opening
   choice and opportunity, trams changing to trolleybuses
then Green Lines and now an express out to the departures lounge
   on the Heath and a joyful urge to fly off to pastures new.

III

Addressing the unknown – that's always been the business of poetry,
   so I've done my stretch with religion, with angels, spirits and the rest,
hoping for the best. Who hasn't drawn alongside a prayer
   watching the news, thinking what if that refugee in Afghanistan
or Iraq were me – and thinking too of the Boat People
   we set out to help, their thanks, their constant smiling, while our own
parents had pulled an empire down about their ears, pirates
   drowning in powerlessness? Meantime, I am rocked by the bus,
raised from wheelchair level, the driver jokes about the weather
   and laughs (*taken our bus lanes, innit*) at Olympians, as he cruises
through the shadow of my grammar school, through tenses, cases, subjects,
   veils and hoods and tattoos, rolling me up to the bus stop.
It's warm in the sun here where there used to be an open-air pool
   and once a Red Cross fete. There's the old air-raid shelter.
Front gardens mainly tarmacked, but privet and laburnum
   and a Boeing to welcome me back to the semi in the cul-de-sac.

Everything seems as it was, even a boy racer's thunderbeat
   feels meant for me, every immigrant face that of family.

IV

No surprise. It's where you were raised, the lost orchard.
   What you're looking for is close, is coming out to reach you
and it's surely not coincidence you stand like a boy engulfed
   by the joy of jet engines at your old house, identifying
ways to take to the air again – to pursue that contrail
   this great monster overhead has lain as it lumbers its way
off to the Rhine or Como or further across the Med
   and up the Nile to Lake Nasser, shooting all the Cataracts
to the Rift Valley, the Indian Ocean, even Zanzibar.
   Yet, red door that I see in dreams so brightly,
you'd say it's home I'm looking for, the winking landing light
   that passes over Prospect Close, the cinder Backway
(hear that old Lexicon card riffling my spokes),
   the Pit, the Sarsen Stone, and the woods at Cranford, secret
yew glades where I made movies, exposed the ghost
   of a stately home, and especially Heathrow: to play on the lifts,
or in the Queen's Building, looking for tail and wing, for exotic
   livery and fruit machines, happy prisoner of my teens.

V

They'll take me in. This is the sound of my earliest childhood.
   Hearing it, it triggers all kinds of half-forgotten instincts.
Yet they are undiminished – in some ways more potent than ever.
   Such treasures, the suns come bursting from the fruit machine.
Yes, the old things are here, an orchard where apples still hang
   but no one is going to pick them, this paradise remains.

And best of all is the discovery of what's been kept safe
    beneath the insulated loft, the rainbow wallpaper,
that reduces me to idiocy. Sheer delight. Another day, then,
    we can go and look at where the garden used to be,
the loganberry cordons, one Spring Bank Holiday, when Dad
    is at home, we can talk about all that's happened and it will come back.
I've weighed up many things since those days and for too long
    have said nothing about my spiritual cultivar, first set
in Heston, Chamberlain's paper airfield, the birthplace of English
    music's most famous unknown, and the source of Elizabeth's
sweet communion manchet; it's time to summon more than
    the metal angels of Heathrow – the immortal ones, and one

VI

I first divined in this house in those early years, whose roof
    was torn off by a plane one night, open in a moment
of renewal and glory to the music of the spheres. As if you could hear
    Hark the Herald broadcast from our candleless piano, scattered
by Mum's fingers across the neck of the banjo to our neighbours,
    inviting them to a secular Christmas, to this essence of family.
As we sit round the table and my father is not like a drunk
    in his diabetic hypo, who should I say thank you to?
Is it God, is there a God? If there is, isn't this too trivial
    for Him to care about? Isn't this in the suburbs of His concerns?
It might be better to be silent, we don't have adequate language,
    make the most of this time between flights, leave the heart to beat.
Yet the right kind of music, the right words, might perhaps
    please or draw a response from skies clogged with ash
that allow presences to draw closer. If we do this,
    the sacrifices that lie under every holidaymaking runway
shouldn't shudder – like it or not, poetry has to absorb
    such painful undertones, internalise them, and let the rest fly.

After Hölderlin: Hyperion's Song of Destiny

Hyperions Schicksalslied

You tread the light fantastic
   on your sprung boards, holy dancers of the soul.
     Heavenly weather teases
       you, its breezes
         like fingertips of a harpist
           drawing sacred scales.

Unmoved by fate as a sleeping
   newborn, the immortal ones breathe
     safely snug
       in their budding, suitably
         aired, their spirits
           eternally
             in flower and their holy eyes
               looking with peaceful
                 clarity for good.

But we have no such luck.
   No chance for the briefest pause,
     unfortunate souls, no –
       we shrink and we tumble
         blindly from one hour
           to the next, water
             flung from precipice to
             precipice, perenni-
               ally down a deeper unknowing.

Under

Crammed up against
the end of the carriage
on the Hammersmith & City,
as we head underground

I hear an amateur
magician passionately
telling the woman he's with
the tricks he's going to do

and as he does, I turn
into The Great Jady
again, with my dark velvet
black-against-black tube

beneath Madame Tussaud's
beyond The Vanishing Arch
towards King's Cross –
in my rucksack, the crowd

glancing at it nervously,
a Life of John Dee –
back through endless parties
and patter and misdirection.

From the Peak

'He had spent the last decade in Manchester... as Warden of the fractious Fellows of the Collegiate Chapter. It was virtual exile.' — Benjamin Woolley, *'The Queen's Conjuror: The Life and Magic of Dr Dee'*

No mobile contact
and Orpheus on the radio

Coming here, as we turned
where it said Elkstones

a pickup hurtled round
the bend and almost –

*

At Roach End, a commemorative plaque
on the stile notes the name of a doctor
'taken' while walking the moors he loved.

He was the age that I am now who walk,
breathe heather, pick, taste, feel
the stain of bilberry, and hope for a signal.

*

The Mermaid Pool no bird
will settle on: the girl
who was drowned there
is serving us with snapper
and marlin; she is dressed
in black and when I remark

on the well that plunges
twenty feet in the corner
of the bar, there's a blink
*Would you like any drink
with that?* They have closed
the room with the view
so the silent landlord can
only watch the road for
errant young farmers
in quest of his pool table.

*

Then there were the two
Methodists who stumbled
around in a local bog
'in the neighbourhood of Leek'
having lost their way
to a meeting where they
hoped to claim souls,
but instead found moss-pits
dragging them to their knees.

*

Lud's Church

the Green Chapel
conceivably

a moss-quilted
fern-vaulted

perpendicular
cleft or gorge

gaiter-deep in
mud and open

to all myths

*

as above, so below

thus I hear Hermes
Trismegistos
whisper across the plains

from here to Huntingdonshire

*

But the story comes back to us
as we hold up our handsets

for network connection, the mother
and daughter freezing here, the thunder,

the drifts, death stealing over them
that Boxing Day, wrapping them in

oblivion. A beep and a message
comes through from Manchester, all well.

*

We sit in this little valley like two
uncut pages of a book by an antiquary
about customs of the Peak. We have
never been read. I begin mid-sentence,
you end mid-sentence. And yet we are

The Silence

So I assumed a double part, and cried
And heard another's voice cry: 'What! are you here?'

Looking into the forest, he looks through a window with bars:
three kinds of bar, then common juniper, spruce, and pine.
He hopes to see something moving there but he seldom can,
except the warder camouflaged, holding a bunch of keys.

Whatever it is that comes out of the forest at night, and calls
or creeps into his dreams and seems to breathe on him or lick
his hand, his ear, is not there now. Now there is work,
the desk, the paper and pen, the glass that he fills, empties, fills.

*

Alone with the pines, their rosiny scent, a breath of self-belief
as they let their bow arms try pizzicato: he is free
to complete a circuit, starting little fires in his head that play
across high boughs, lift low cobwebs, drift.

He hums, he mutters, he grasps at old fungus and moss and kex
and catches the gist of a point the black woodpecker made as it passed.
This is where it will be found, the substance that has no taste
but once touched will never go away. This is what takes

him out: this breath of an ember of a final chance of making a start.
The trees let down their guard, become like spokes on an ancient wheel,
though a wheel that's going nowhere. Stuck. Imagining himself on a real
wagonful of timber, he lights up, and believes in the art

of getting something somewhere. It's not enough simply to carve
your name in bark. You might as well sculpt Venus out of snow.
The process is more mysterious. It's a case of managing to break through
drifts of nothing; something you thought you saw from the cart and swerved

to avoid, and now – look, you're moving again, the drayhorse
taking the strain over cone and needle, up the dry track.
To be both the man on the cart and the horse, to be the one who'll make
a desk from the wood, and the one who'll sit at it confronting chaos.

*

Motherless, fatherless, he looks into the silence and reaches deep
through that solitude for what he can find. The impression is of slime
and at the same time of something sticking to his fingers at each grim
attempt to pull it out, whatever it is. With a kind of swooping

glissando, it slides towards him. At last, the long unnatural coma
is stirring to a hum, hypnotically. Now, with one tremendous final
tug it's free, and he is free. *Ariel*, it sings – as the pine
tree's lips close – and louder sings, pure amber.

*

Nothing in it but an example of a lost species. Wings spread
as if to fly, but no hope of that. He was fooled
into thinking the new might be presented in the glow of the old.
If he could set it free, he would; meanwhile, the world will applaud.

*

As they all do, gliding into the station, walking to the house,
angling for endorsement. He looks up from his work and briefly scowls,
but he softens quickly enough. All artists are willing gulls
who want to be liked, to be promoted. And he has no excuse:

apart from the gathering banks of unanswered mail, there's nothing else
but this great empty sky – though there go the swans again
on their nightly circuit. Sometimes he stands and dreams of going down
to join that creature he set afloat in the underworld on hell's

unrippled lake, where only the hiss of surface noise disturbs…
and it's as if he stands beside a cataract on the Upper Nile
in the shadow of a barrage keeping the flow back, restraining the annual
inundation. There are the tops of temples, that sacred cobra's

desperate lunge is to save a pharaonic reputation
from the electric chair. Beneath the muddy modernising waters
outstretched eagle wings in amber await a better future.
Above them here his visitors are worried. They ask the question.

But he has had dynasties to prepare for this. 'Too much light'
he tells them, 'is bad for art.' The swan prefers to glide beneath
the earth, and sacred works are happy holding their breath
until the sun comes out and asks them to play, or not.

*

Like an airship it hangs there, or something beginning with Z
that preaches the last as if it were the first. And then it will be
a dumbbell waiting for him to lift. The impossibility.
Or an unending Grand Prix that happens in Möbius's head.

It represents bulk. A figure of light. An egg with a knot
tied in it. The number Pythagoras did not count,
that God believed beyond Him. It is also a stylish antique
golden torc that he would like to wear tonight when out

at his eighth reception at eight o'clock, when eight times eight
enthusiasts will ask what he is working on. He'll be forced
to say it's finished, to say it's not started, to say he tossed
the damn thing in the fire, to hell with the Muses and Beethoven.

*

'It's all rhythm,' he says. 'Once you get that you can't go wrong.'
Yet though he is ready for the wave, the upsurge, nothing moves.
Try carving. Try modelling. Patiently he looks out. His reflection heaves
in the glassy calm, knowing that once the Oceanides have sung

you are alive again, if you can catch that wave, control it,
rise enough to reach what's in the air, in the single movement.
The man that hath no music in him, all he has is the pavement
grey, a ringing in his ears, the clock, his gun and geese in the violet

evening sky, chaos shimmering behind their v of order
honking its way to success. Send your dog to collect the bag,
hold them up proudly, imitate their cry. Canada or greylag
or snow goose. Share another round with your friends to celebrate the
    murder.

The artist knows what really flies as he dreams and thinks and creates
simultaneously, and muscles know it as he strains to reach
greater lengths and sees the scarp and floats over its edge
above the plain, the ordinary. Until then, he patiently starts

to rake dead leaves, back, forth, back, forth,
physical effort. Anything but contemplating that frozen sheet
where something underneath might be alive. Not long to wait
before cold sets in for good. When he'll ask if it's worth

throwing a pebble on to the ice to listen for that strange warble,
electronic, minatory, and modern. Or should he go spinning
happy lines on it all winter? Listen to the rondo and the warning
cry of geese, and throw it again, again, the magic pebble.

*

Thirteen times the surgeon reached into his throat, a route
that might even lead to his genius, or his belly – which is forbidden
drink for the next seven years. The river banks widen
and still no sea for the estuary. 'I've got it!' comes the shout.

*

The fear throughout had been of dying before he reached the end,
not this prolonged epilogue, slow countdown to the launch, strike,
or revelatory orbit. Across the airwaves, icy talk.
Between east and west, in his personal No Man's Land

he picks a way. Better to be silent than join in the puffing
of mushroom politics. He contents himself with the forest floor where real
finds proliferate, peacefully, though mantraps and old mines are concealed.
And once it's dark, he'll try again. Of course, the universe is laughing

but he's ready, five oak beams beneath him and a carpet worn
threadbare in the drag of his pacing. East. West. No one to advise
on choosing the right phrase for making suns, planting stars.
An elk strolls by his window. His hand shakes. Get it down.

*

The bear who has slept a long time begins now and again to wake.
He is in the mountains. Searching the soul's infinite recesses.
This is what he hears. Väinämöinen, who surpasses
all human achievement with the knowledge he found on the shore of the
    lake.

*

Had he persevered, put up with those humiliating assaults
on mastery, he might have danced to a different tune. But virtuosity,
like virtue, is dull. He was, you could say, a maestro of anxiety,
sensing kernels, live shells, as he played. Never the sun-vaults

and high fits of one that holds the treasure he firmly knows
to be his between a shoulder and a cheek. Spruce, hard maple.
Ebony. Never the adored and bushy-tailed star pupil
of the master of veneer and varnish, protected, preserved, one of those

who know the value of balancing hard against soft, choosing timber
from the leeward side of the spotlit holy mountain, where the snows
run out, to ensure the rings are close and even. One of those
who go before the world with nothing but their surface, remembered

ever after for their depths. The rain plucks out a humoresque
on the lake beyond his door. Back to the five-string devil's dance
he's scraped his soul into to fit the circus ring. Silence
broken by hell's bells. Dullness. That unyielding desk.

*

'So, write for the circus. Here comes that tightrope walker
of a theme to thrill the children. Now show them how you can tame the roar
with a glockenspiel, how a solitary trombone will swallow fire,
how knives may be thrown at a minor. And don't forget to knock

a dominant cop on his keynote as the Viennese clowns tumble into
the big top you put up for them. While above you, a jazz
trapeze is swinging, and hanging by her sweet Parisian knees:
the muse of the circus. The place is abuzz. And you're the one who sent

the poor devils up there. Encore? Clowns in a burning church
with buckets of pure cold water. The hilarity! The cries of delight –
and amazement that you hadn't offered this before, instead
of that gloomy show at Highbrow Hall. Let the gladiators march!'

*

It is as if he were trying to engrave an epic on a hazel shell
or dance to steps tapped out by sap in a deciduous wood,
the kind they have in England, where he is at home and understood,
broad-leaved, broad-minded, trusting what you feel.

*

Good morning, England. The mirror replies, a courteous host
whose silver is wearing thin, whose views incline to emphasise
port and pudding. He weighs up which of the various different ties
will match his swan-white suit, and now descends, the Guest,

to Georgian London, royalty, oysters, Rosa and Sir Henry Wood.
They press his weak hand. They snatch at his coat. How people love
his work here – and love to copy it, though he can hardly disapprove
except when they make of it some gilt-edged drifting cloud

and moonshine nonsense, as if the very highest art were varnish.
English artists, much as he loves them, lack a vital spark,
internal compulsion to bring out their enigma from the back
of all those sideboards they inherited. It's not about the finish.

*

'Stop worrying and get on with your work! Perhaps you will live
for a long time yet.' No drinking. No smoking.
And a roomful at the restaurant who never tire of joking
'How will you manage without your usual fuel?' What he wouldn't give.

*

Every time a rival succeeds, something that was greening withers.
Yes, he has had his share of triumphs, but that's all in the past
and artists prefer now. You never know if this is your last
word or where the next will come from. If there are to be others,

will they equal those by A, whose name is always screaming
from the papers, or B who has been invited to write a work
for C (a national treasure) or D (a knight). While in New York,
E and F have announced their movie. As for this latest beaming

G-force he has to endure, at least it's clear there's nothing there,
though no one tells the Emperor. There's something to be said for keeping
    mum
when all around are fawning. Better to decline, stay at home,
get something *right*, not caring whether the critics cheer.

*

Self-criticism, that's what it comes down to: knowing where
to make the cut, having the courage to leave something out
and an instinct for a buried seed. The pampered, brightly coloured pet
flies solo from its cage, round the house, perching here

and there. Everyone shouts 'Close the windows!' But no, wait.
let it go. It was only whistling what you wanted to hear,
what you had taught it to repeat. Locate that hoard instead, and lure
these other birds, the drab ones hopping outside, hoping to eat.

*

All artistic enterprise is a ride through the night towards
a sunrise that may never come, a dawn chorus uncertain
whether to strike up for spring or ring down the curtain
on silence. Thunder-sparking, he has cantered too many decades.

Bubbling clouds hang over the east. A sliver of lament
on a single string hovers, flaps, then vanishes. In his throat
something grows that knows what it wants to say about
this remorseless place he has reached; about the gaudy circus tent

collapsed in a heap, the dung and spoors of show-creatures who broke
free, the abandoned tubas, wigs and powder tossed in the wind
as it rises more and more fiercely ready for some un-
deniable, unprecedented storm. He knows he must take a break.

A mouth is opening on the smoky horizon to tell him so, although
it has no voice, tilting a bottle of red wine
before him and offering heavenly oysters, seven, eight, nine,
until he reels to a halt. If you sneak a look, catch that low

barbed-wire gaze, between his eyebrows you will see
five wrinkles and some wisps of creation dancing there.
But do not try to talk to him. Armies are still advancing there
on a grim mission to the reddening east, a scorched earth policy.

*

Sixty thousand grey autumn lakes and a greeting from the master,
who says: find your own form, let your creative thoughts,
the way they take spiritual shape, determine how the lots
fall, the pieces of the mosaic. Improvise. Make beauty of disaster

and tragedy of utter bliss. Take the turn of the year with you
and when you think of bells, let posterity decide if they're even
bells or something lighter, more silvery. Be ready for the raven,
the waves, bluish grey, a splash of sun, the cold white cliffs,

a scarred landscape, and there towards the forested, patrolled horizon,
revolution's border. Step in his boat, the moon rippling,
a steady motion. Everything grieves. But he persists, grappling
with nevermore. The pieces fall before him as he rows on.

*   *   *

Absolute silence. Although his children play, see friends,
have homework and practice to do, everything gives way to his work.
America demands and he must answer. Nobody is allowed to talk
as his throat pulses. Peace. At least until winter ends.

*

When he was unable to speak, he watched two elk pass
so close to the house he could have reached out – but instead
he found two of his five daughters to embrace. They are allowed
to roam free, but know theirs are the lines on which Papa's

patient gaze is fixed. They eat and lick salt and offer
the rough edge of their tongue, swim, dive, are crowned
monarchs of their home. When he was unable to speak, they learned
to draw quietly, to abstain from piano practice, would hover

outside his room. No one wanted to speak. When the phone
rang he ripped it from the wall in a rage and bull-charged
head down out of his door. Later, camouflaged,
crestfallen, under the shadow of a winter moon

he looks in on his girls, whispering their way to sunrise,
to bring them food, and hear as he quietly turns to his writing
their intimate voices browse exotic places, share exciting
dreams of that wild, grown-up world, and all its lunacies.

*

A white-suited spectre, he walks up to his favourite seat
and inspects the landscape. In plain winter sun he simply dazzles,
a presence declaring its territory, warbler among the hazels.
He puzzles over what it was he glimpsed as he stood to greet

his wife when she came downstairs, or as he tuned the wireless
to hear that commemorative broadcast, or while he was at the piano…
frames flick by, their specks of dirt and light a continuo
playing as if from the window of a train he is being carried in, fearless

towards the future. Birch, pine, alder. Through a wicket gate
and he's off the heath, back into his thirty years of forest
where every conceivable composition is nesting somewhere, the nearest
storm-battered, the farthest a scrub of lightweight saplings, fit

for domestic consumption only. The man in the white suit, turning
the leaves of his work in his head, a tight smile at his lips and a cigar
unlit before him, thinks what vain creatures we mortals are,
nature will always outwit us, and yet we go on learning.

*

The arctic fox is about again, starting fires in the sky,
spraying up snow with its brush, another frustrated artist:
he hopes to sell them in the capital, where he will creep in his latest
disguise to negotiate with galleries. Someone has to pay.

*

The children open their Advent Calendar. The first day of December
shows a donkey, the second a shepherd, and so on until we reach
the eighth, which will be his umpteenth birthday. He stands nearby to watch
as they open it. A fragment of piano music. But what's in a number?

God's door opens for a moment, and angels are singing *him*.
The notes form up on paper, like boys on the western front.
Earth and worms and heartache won't stop the raid, can't
avoid a stalemate. Wave after wave. No good. Yet a form

the honest artist may with luck and hard work uncover
hides beneath the bloody mess, a raw material from worlds
brutally broken up – dig, it's a kind of clay and it moulds
the shape, the shape you're after, the shape of when war is over.

*

December's wan smile. Dark and full of poetry. The work
goes forward, large or small. A woodcock roasting in the oven.
A movement warming in the head. Sleigh rides. And thirty-seven
pages of a masterpiece. Christmas. News of a fresh attack.

*

'When foreigners visit us it's invariably the silence they remark on.
Out here, but in the cities too. A reticent people.
Clean, calm; followers of rules, not of a timetable.
Proud, but self-effacing, accustomed to purple days that darken

and lighten but will not reach true night, and to our nights
that never see day. They say we don't smile, shade
the sun from our lives, shunning its directness, unwilling, even afraid
to look at (let alone speak to) strangers. This defeats

those who do not understand how we enjoy the silence.
No need to fill in gaps in a conversation.
No need to provide irrelevant information.
Avoiding small talk is in our nature and it's not insolence

to halt a discussion in its tracks – the way I like to end a piece
unceremoniously, without warning, a shrug –
any more than it is to answer 'How are you?' with a log
of Seasonal Affective Disorders. Silence means what it says.'

*

They lose his work, forget him, then find it, remember at last to review him
and say he has dressed folksong in a toga, he's a craftsman not a master.
Their comments lodge in his head, in its darkest, loneliest cells, and fester
or burst in a fury of accusation. Will anyone ever know him?

In a place that is simply nowhere, separate, overlooked, its language
disconnected, its people only known to themselves, he waits
for the spark from heaven. This winter there are plenty of notable lights
but none call him: they fall in Russian here or there in English.

*

His face frozen in a block of white pocked stone, a mask,
an icy gargoyle, the march (from *Eroica?)* enforces slow motion.
Daffodils anticipate their fanfare in a new plantation
of blazing candles. It is a dream. Yet he dare not risk

wresting himself from stone to greet those laying a wreath
or reading an elegy, a eulogy, the famous voices,
but senses a barely controllable burgeoning, unreckoned forces
of fugal bud and bloom. He coughs, he chokes, he begs for breath

in his sleep, but there is none within this thick white stone
where a long black line of lovers moves in perpetual
ostinato motion past the flowers. So many people,
and he alone beneath the climbing, blossoming big tune.

*

Beyond the crescent he can make out the moon's globe, entire
and blood-red. It's good to be reminded that it survives
as a body of work survives beyond the shrinking sliver
today would see, if today ever left its comfortable fire.

*

They merely want to be sent a few records or need his advice
on their marriage plans, or feel they can easily improve on what he's
    done,
(*herewith, my new version*). He sees the best in his fellow man.
Each letter represents a life. He imagines each voice

(*has cum to mi atenshun evry singl theam yu yusd
mi pursenal propperty, yor world fame bin acheevd
at spence of mi effurts*), can hear them, the poor, the sick, the unloved,
this one with a flying saucer photo and this who has enclosed

examples of his genius, others who demand he instantly send
his latest manuscript for their collection, or require his autograph
for their six-year-old who adores his work. Ah, so much love
from the wide, wide world. And here in silence he tries to command

the phases of the moon. Today, a wordless beggar appeared at the door
all cuts and bruises. He gave him food, his own old clothes,
and sent him on his way the spitting image. The night breathes.
He turns to his slippers, positions them by the bed with loving care.

*

When shadows begin to shorten and critics peep out from their den,
the future pales, failure has stolen its colour. Five swans
are on the ice. He watches them with binoculars. And at once
spring seems to break in him. He feels sixteen again.

Swans are white notes in the Dorian mode and glide above
pure cold water; winter is dominant; a sixth, a seventh
seeking resolution. Lines in the ice appear. Strength
returns, crackling creativity. Waters start to move.

*

Yes, it must change. The original must go. A dawn assault?
Too many casualties. A night raid then. His ears
ache from barrage, theme, countertheme. Everything blurs
to waste land. He makes a cut that will determine the result.

*

All night the sound of trees falling from the weight of snow.
What are they trying to tell him? They know it can all be too much,
the bearing of silence, its transfiguring power. And now the futile search
across a snowfield, following tracks, finding a hopeful spoor

that leads nowhere. Here, his six ways meet, converge
into a single path beyond the drift: a tree falls with a
crumbling, crumpling thud (it is the only sound) and further
into the dream he emerges at a clearing. The site of a forge.

He imagines the blaze within, the anvil, the hiss of red shoes
kissing water, but above all the hammer, hammer, hammer.
Silence will not acknowledge this, does not remember
a blacksmith, his smallest spark. It has eliminated every noise.

* * *

A furious row. Sometimes he thinks they ought to separate
until Diogenes wheels his wartime searchlight round and shows
precisely where he's gone wrong. Then picks out a dazed
creature wandering in the desert, where it's been fasting, where it

has been forgotten since its birth. Look how it squats
on Hatchet Mountain, his bastard Fourth, skinny saint, fed
four times a day by the devil. The glockenspiel ahead
rings in another year. *Con sordini*. (Mutes).

*

'Unless his drinking destroys us first, his work is my sacred mission.
That I had to lower myself when I married him I do not resent
though others delight in reminding me. Such values hardly count –
his work does, our children – in the face of this social revolution.

Lives have been smashed apart. But we are free. Gently I knock
and bring him his tea (he hides the bottle he thinks I haven't seen).
'Liberty, equality, fraternity,' he smiles, laying down his pen
and listening to what I tell him about the flags in town to mark

our new president's return, about machine-gun fire
raking the capital. I also mention my health. But he has to work
on what's light, saleable (revisions to his masterpiece must wait), while dark
clouds gather over our house. We do not go out for fear

of what might happen (my brother spoke in support of the people
and found himself in a prison cell with six prostitutes).
There's much I do not tell him because he has to clear our debts.
He calls it slavery. I comment instead on the early morning's purple

skyline and remind him that a lovely leg of smoked lamb has been sent
by an *a capella* singer he knows. Our silver wedding is soon
but too much is uncertain. I leave him working on his own.
To work in peace is all he wants. All any of us want.'

*

Partridge he loves. And grasshoppers. Swallows' nests. He hates
that taste of metal. Today he buries himself in a full
page picture of a winter landscape, and says he can smell
the snow, distinctly. He cannot bear to touch cotton sheets.

*

A chess game carries on around him: he won't discuss
White moves or Red, though they'll shout 'When are you going to write
something for us?' and he'll offer a marching miniature from his kit,
not what they need. He cannot fight. At the edge of the ice

white birds are rocked by waves. Safe in his head,
the Fifth, the Sixth, the Seventh. Elsewhere, a black and endless war
without opus number. Ideology has no cure.
But nor has art. Miniatures, miniatures. Debts must be paid.

*

Smoke rings above the *Wienerwald*, where a voice proclaims:
'I don't comment on his work because I don't understand it.'
Infinite repeatability means that what has ended
can always start again. 'Tighten the ring road,' it hums.

*

Red on White in the squares of the capital. Here, terrified women.
The young ones get on his nerves. But how can he send them out
into this red blizzard to play red snowballs? He hears a shot
and writes a tranquil phrase, goes about whispering in German.

There have been death threats. Within the circle of their sun they're free
and warm, however: three degrees and nature weirdly abundant.
The wooden sledge he bought for the children is useless now, abandoned
outside the house, beside those bloody spots from their rowan tree.

Now here come the snow men, marching in, demanding passes,
raiding their storeroom for carrots and coal, searching the place for
	weapons.
But they never ask the crucial question. Or touch, as it happens,
those final revisions on his desk, their hidden overwhelming forces.

*

As if any of this matters. Appease the gods with fine cigars.
Gaze at the night and its absent moon. While, for art, forget it,
and wonder instead about his hair. Perhaps he should simply cut it
off to a parody of Nero or one of Hollywood's fading stars.

*

Press on to the lake and the mute swans gathered at the end,
out of reach, but ready to fly, given the word – if only
he knew the word. He feels he is being watched: the steady, sternly
attentive eye of something hidden that has colonised his private land.

Let them do their silent dance on the pin in his head where he's hung
music like a mighty glacier, high and ready to move, mould
everything ready for survival. He feels himself grow old
with every scratch he makes. He sees himself take the wrong

path, prints cross and overlap, go back where they began.
The angel-swans float on as ever inaccessible
to him or hunters, poachers, soldiers; unless the impossible
flypast happens, the vision; the completion of the Aristotelian chain.

*

To forge musical metalwork and fashion sonorities of silver.
Never let go of the sublime, even when the corpse
bobs up from the bottom of the lake, and there go your hopes.
The gate clangs behind you. Look at your head on a royal salver

as the world waltzes. But the metallic taste remains. You cannot speak
because these coins are on your tongue, bomb-blocking your throat,
and even when you've prised them out and into the nearest slot,
all that they play is… The rod bends, bends but does not break.

*

An arm reaches, holding a handwritten message, sealed,
which he ignores. On the shore, he sees something floating,
an empty whisky bottle, one of his. It contains a note
etched on bark. He knows the hand. But he will not be told:

flings a stone, kicks a tree. If he wishes to have a drink
why shouldn't he? And if she wishes to stay at home
instead of attending his premiere… The rocks around him begin to hum,
their carvings spell it out, the same words he thought he'd sunk,

a habit he thought he'd kicked: it drips on to the forest floor
and turns to rosin, bitter, clear. 'Do not rely on spirits
or you will lose me.' Now it's the wood nymph. What he creates
she monitors from the shadows, a message he can't ignore.

*

A funeral march, he heard it half a century too soon,
drum, cymbals and a bronze bust that seemed to say here
is all you came to. But coming to the mountains, a bear
danced its ceremonial death, and music there was none.

*

He trembles. It will not stop, yet three great works remain
standing while half the world is rubble. Their all-clear sounds
above the concentration camps. He trembles. It never ends,
the climb to the cone. Lava, ash, fire in the very rain.

Will he pass the third gate? Another kingdom, migration
of refugees, of cranes, their oboe cries. Something special
for his finale, *adagio*? After all, adversity is a measure
of strength. He goes on. He will survive, as will his nation.

*

The friend who, more than anyone, helped him on his way, is dead.
He did not see enough of him, but there they are at a table
at lunch still, picking over the day's specials: comfortable
reputations spiked, dangerous dissident voices freed.

No one was listening. As if they'd sat on a tiny stepping stone
while the waters (and the waiters) hurried past. All he can hear
now is the creak of a wax cylinder that was not there
to catch his table talk. He died too young. The hand has gone

that guided their art: illuminations in a grave black script
are sorry for not having written, accompany a book, a cutting,
and always praise his work, before that final Christmas greeting.
As the rest of the world was singing its heart out, his just stopped.

*

'The pause before…' another friend observed, 'a sudden rest,
or break – as here – in a closed circuit, constitute the very core
of what we create, become the thing in itself. In fact, there's more
to be found in silence than in sound, which lacks its elasticity.'

*

'*Mirabile*, not to say *horribile dictu,* it is done.
In its final form. I have fought with God.' His hands quiver
so he can scarcely write. If only his dear friend were alive,
not breathing at the frosted window. Freezing point. Sun.

No crystal can guide him. He has cut the last two thirds.
'Keep the opening.' He rubs his hands. 'It's where it all began.'
The frost remains. He has only seen wild geese, no swan
or any other migratory bird. But suddenly, as if he heard

the call of the original, distant, strange. Quick, before it's off
to the publisher, restore it all, revise, revise the ending again,
its shape emerging clear at last. He lays down his pen.
'God knows He and I have wrestled long enough.'

* * *

She watches over him, an English gardener. Before their farewell,
as she asks for an autographed picture – no thanks, no dedication, 'no need
for words between us' – he might have seen some shoot, perhaps a bud
of what she calls 'tendresse', confessing to a feeling 'neither shallow

nor wanting in propriety'. Counting the hours, she says he can count on her
whatever's in store, if it be more 'great and beautiful works'
(as she believes), or whether that craze of tiny hairline cracks
fracturing, lets in the smoke and drink… 'it will have no effect on our

friendship', and all that binds a lover of art to her favourite artist.
'I've waited for you to break through; now the moment has almost come.
But don't waste your energies. Your new marching orders for the summer:
to write (no drinking, no America, no trivialities), to write your greatest.'

*

'Worked. Felt life's richness today and the power of my writing.'
Rain streams down. On his desk a glass of water.
The tap drips in the bathroom. Somewhere one of his daughters
is crying inconsolably. Beyond her, the world is waiting.

*

At the castle gate, then inside plotting his way out
along its haunted landing – the same every night. Who is it
chasing him through those heavy doors to that high window, dizzy
invitation? Art has to be dreamed as well as thought,

a kind of waltz, a lovemaking, and if you can't achieve
that doubleness, there's no point in standing at the barbican
hoping to pull drawbridge and portcullis up again.
Forget the dance. Just watch the sky at night. Or maybe wave

to a girl in the park who's lost her wedding ring, her crown, who's lost
in your dream enough to share a few steps to the muffled source
of true enchantment... Who is it at that high window? Of course,
he recognises Don Juan, waiting for the stone guest.

*

Now he's reached an age where it's not remarkable to die,
he thinks of Haydn falling on his knees each day to ask for strength
to finish *The Creation*, of Bruckner (ditto) for his (unfinished) Ninth.
He himself laboured through six. And on the seventh day...

*

In a single arc the stone he had hurled rose and fell, skipping
unexpectedly three times as it hit the frozen lake
and made three times a low growling solo like
a trombone beneath the ice. All his life he had been hoping

for this moment, to achieve this one perfect accurate throw,
like a cricketer, a game of which he knows nothing but white
against green and a stillness at its heart. Why create
when you could play games? Because it felt to him as though

he flew for twenty minutes through the space between his hand
and the surface of the lake, like a swan, but more like humanity
itself released for the duration of the flight. As if eternity
were from here to there, in his own garden, icebound.

*

One daughter is leaving home. She has her own career
and plays piano with devotion, although she (his little sprite)
will only ever write to mummy. The others marry or migrate
on beating wings, leaving this bundle of sticks without a fire.

*

He drinks his coffee, puts his chair in front of the wireless, and tries
twiddling the knobs to find some music: only whistling or Morse
or distant jazz, no, useless. So he steps backwards
to the chair, the chair that has been moved, and falls through the place

where the wall used to be where now there is a sandy shore's
broad expanse, waves beating time, Italian sun,
and two girls walking, talking along the strand – gone
as he drops back into time and on to the living room floor,

everyone leaping up to save him. The man is over ninety.
But not dead this time, not even unconscious, laughing loudly
on the carpet and entirely unhurt, indeed (he says) he hardly
noticed the change of worlds, his brief brush with infinity.

*

Rejection he's learnt to accept: a curt refusal or 'it's with regret…',
the coming to terms with the silence – are they bent on ignoring you
or just too busy to respond? Harder is learning to, bearing to
criticise what you love the most, and make that cut.

*

A stranger comes to the door. Odd verses, gestures, runes
he cannot follow or fathom – he's teetering still on a crucial phrase
of his work, no time, but as the door slams shut, a noise
outside, a plucking, starts, like a harp made out of fish bones.

Magic powers the land, for all the promises of a cable draped
above the tree tops: those stories will never grow dim.
Of how a wizard will stick a knife in your mast for a tot of rum,
command the sea, the sky. That phrase, where is it? But his table top

has lost anchor, a weird wind drives him, drum-
drumming demonically from the roof-tree, swamps echoing,
earth collapsing every last standing stone: a reckoning.
And no one home to save him from his own *in memoriam*.

*

'Lie there my art,' he says, and speaks to his remaining daughter
about the shipwreck. It is an illusion. Everything will be well,
he promises, though the curtain went up on a vision of hell
and high water. What she saw was merely the dramatic part of

a larger whole: she must listen to understand what that might be,
processes of redemption, settling of scores, the balancing of a spirit level
to carry the weight of the world's collected volumes of learning, evil
snug against good, earth to air, waking with sleep.

*

He holds them spellbound, look, the seven of them, horseshoed
downstage by the director, and each in a grey crumpled outfit
with a shabby hat. He is the only one whose dark suit
looks well cut, the only one in polished shoes

and wearing a Homburg. They are all men, and looking at him
in amusement ('Beseech you sir, be merry, you have cause, so have
we all, of joy') as his right hand blurs in a vigorous wave
of an upbeat. He knows who's the rightful heir. In the abysm

of darkness behind them powers lurk, among those inky leaves,
perhaps a critic. What are they waiting for? Vienna to bring
its chopped woods? A Masque of Peace? Or some unearthly voice to sing
strange messages of art's end and the relief approval gives?

*

Curlew rises from an A, bullfinch double-stops on D,
pheasants clatter their shutters, starlings show what they've learnt
from factory sirens and now the phone rings. *If you want
to see the cranes,* it squawks, *they've come.* And he has gone to see.

*

'Widespread they stand, the Northland's dusky forests,' and smoke drifts
from deep within them, a top secret clearing where a man has paused
to light his cigar and launch his genius again. Furrows, crazed
as the bark of *pinus sylvestris*, eyes down, and something lifts

off his smooth domed head, gathering needles and mushrooms
into its cloud: the cold bone of creation thrown to a Russian
spaceship with a dog inside who longs for a tree, her solo mission
howling for the moon, 'ancient, mysterious, brooding savage dreams'.

*

Every day he pushes the envelope aside, leaves a new
emptiness and silence. Those you grew up with, they disappear
into the mouth that has nothing to say but will eventually devour
even Tapio's war whoop. The forest believes in you.

*

A drunken butler, he staggers across the room and leans against
the green brick chimney, as if he were happier there, his wife
reading with the children at the table, ignoring him. The low roof
lowers its five staves menacingly. He needs to get his hands

on a bottle of something. Now he plays the jester. Again, ignored,
he becomes instead the mooncalf, the ignorant poet-monster
sprinkling abuse on all his critics, whom he threatens to murder
with a log. But first possess their books. They say not a word,

child, wife, those masqueraders, as he slopes back to his cell
to contemplate the problem. In an instant he's turned magician again,
and can summon spirits. At his command they will cast disdain on any
whose only gift is to shake a thunder sheet or act the fool.

*

Breezily, the American presses him for details – 'Folks at home
would find it of the greatest interest' – but the face has already begun
    to harden
with a cracking sound *Ich kann nicht*, the blank expanse broadening.
No vessel, no icebreaker can hope to get through to him.

*

To soft music, enter the shapes again, and dance with mocks
and mows holding up fragments of his writing. There goes the harpy
transformed to a swan. It works, it works. Those who were happy
are brought low, the depressed are raised. His high charm works.

Here it is. Long requested. Promised to the USA.
Here before him. 'Please don't bind the copy yet.
Still working on it. Pure youthfulness.' And what
though his hands tremble, his hearing goes, and people say

it sounds like that because he is old… By this age, all the greats
were long dead. Nobody is expected to produce half decent work
once they reach the middle stretch. You're past it. Time for a walk
to the lake, the geese laying their golden eggs, among other feats.

*

But oh the sinking in his stomach, the nerves, the rack, as he imagines
taking the stage. Boils erupt, muscles knot, the audience
is growing restless. Let him not be one of those shapes who dance
and sing and smile. Let him remain invisible master of the pageant.

*

No television. He has never seen a talkie, has never
travelled on a bus, let alone a plane. Yet the older he grows
the more he wants to see what is ahead, with open eyes
face the strange trends of the age. He tells his silent driver

how a famous airman once invited him to cross the Alps
on a special mission, what could go wrong? He longed to say yes
to this rare chance, risk-free, but said no, and when news
came of the crash, there were no survivors. 'Except me.' It helps

to believe (he says) it was for a purpose (a swig from his flask): he wants
to build an altar on the bare rock there above his house,
a gesture to the Ultimate Being, he says, to whatever Higher Powers
control his life, to acknowledge humanity's (and art's) meaning for once.

'Even this weak sunshine – miraculous,' he says, 'the peace and devotion
it stirs, as if a law in the universe, some inconceivable
harmony, made every human effort puny, laughable.'
He says: 'That's my idea of God. The artistic logic in creation.'

*

The cranes are off on their long journey south, grey skeins
passing over the house. He hurries to the veranda. Their wingbeats
and their trumpeting *krooh, krr.* Suddenly, one crane separates
from the v and swings low over him. He knows what it means.

*

Grey chocolate depresses him. And venison soup with juice
of blackcurrants. He hates that blue bank note on the table.
But he loves this red silk cloth. 'Imagine you could travel
to Mars, imagine the colours there, the music.' Strange how he knows

when something he's written is on the air. He is sitting reading
when he'll turn restless, stalk across the room, turn the controls
and there it will be… Again and again he tunes into the soul's
strange synchronicities, recognising places, noting

facts he could not know about people, even anticipating
the number of years he has left. 'How childish to delude ourselves
our tiny brains have grasped it all.' Behind glass, the shelves
of honours, medals, orders. When the past comes, he will be waiting.

*

'I'm going to the inevitable.' Slowly he leaves the table and the cliché
accompanies him, its feet paddling furiously beneath the mirrored
calm of the surface like the mother in the painting of the myth, as if she'd
    carried
him here with the strength in that tree-trunk arm: it seems to push

down even as her face stares up in clenched defiance.
The swan looks on from the far corner of the frame, upstaged, and mute
as she is, and he – stretched out, the remnants of his genius, the poetry
and music in him, extracted (blood on the stones) and left to science.

*

The meteorite is made of papier-mâché. The bears and wolves are stuffed.
The men are noble and peaceful and poetic. The women have nothing to say.
And so we all experience the culture of the land of a thousand lakes.
An icebreaker. A tar pit. Some fisheries. The Friends of Handicraft.

*

'Here silence speaks,' he says, and falls silent again.
The interviewer persists. 'What advice would you give to the young?'
'Everything must be necessary. Everything must live.' A long
pause, before 'Do you have a favourite?' How could he explain?

Generality and depth; inevitability. But also economy and
the unexpected. Listening to a broadcast, he heard his White Dwarf
humming its distance and its destiny. A new probe went off
towards the eighth planet, but God knows where it will end.

'Have there been recent successes?' So it goes on and on.
He says how he likes to tune in to the radio, to the new works,
that he sees a great future for his country and its artists. The green bricks
glisten above the fireplace; in the grate there is nothing left to burn.

*

'I haven't written before as I didn't want to disturb your peace,
but I'm planning the season already and wonder whether the work,
which we all await with great impatience in Boston and New York,
will be ready for the spring? I understand you never like to discuss

what's only in your head, but since you have spoken of it as 'complete'…
We hope to present your works in sequence, culminating in this.
If you can tell me its length and what would sit well with it, please?
The papers are keen to announce it. Can we settle on a date?'

*

In seven languages he says nothing. The work is never complete.
But in his sleep his arms keep moving to the music of a dream.
The same two pages always. It will happen in time,
he reassures them, it will emerge, you simply have to wait.

*

Cranes fly across his twilight, turn to enemy planes,
out to bomb him. He reaches in his sleep for one of Beecham's pills
and wakes to a sound from another room that reminds him of turntables
squeaking to be fed what he has not yet produced; the artist leans

towards the radio and hears familiar strains and a voice announce
that at a quarter past nine this evening, peacefully,
and in his own bed… He laughs out loud, blissfully
aware his friends and family are there, that the cranes and geese and
    swans

have flown and he is with them, beating, working, still creating
as they carry him, as they bury him, pushing on through time
to achieve that last great something, released now from his fame –
its tidal wave, the keys, the bars, the waste – to go on writing.

Notes

Nebamun's Tomb

This sequence of poems was written after visiting the British Museum to see their newly revived Egyptian collection, in particular the paintings from the tomb of an accountant called Nebamun. These remarkable works of art, dating from around 1350 BC, were 'removed' and sold to the museum by the British consul-general in Egypt, Henry Salt (1780–1827), a keen and well-placed collector of antiquities. My own interest in Egypt began rather later, between 1979 and 1981, when my wife and I were volunteer teachers in Aswan, an experience which resulted in *Westerners* (Hippopotamus Press, 1982), my first collection. For some of the detail in the sequence, I have drawn on Richard Parkinson's invaluable guide, *The Painted Tomb-Chapel of Nebamun*, published by the British Museum Press (2008).

From the Peak

Originally much longer, this was written during a short stay in the Peak District while our younger daughter was on a piano course at Chetham's Music School, site of the old College of Priests. I did not know at the time of John Dee's connection with Chetham's (the library has many of his profusely annotated books), yet that week I was for some reason immersed in the literature of the occult. Perhaps it was the presence of Lud's Church (possibly Gawain's Green Chapel) which our other daughter had just been visiting for a Simon Armitage film she was involved with. At any rate, it was a week of strange interconnected happenings, not least when early one morning in Leek before the shops were even open, Jane and I bumped into the Methodist minister who had married us thirty years previously.

The Silence

Sibelius lived with his family at Ainola, their house in Järvenpää, Finland until he was over ninety, by which time he was world's most famous living composer – indeed, when an American addressed an envelope with nothing but 'Jean Sibelius, Europe', the letter promptly reached him. But he released virtually no music from his forest home for the last thirty years of his life after his incidental music for *The Tempest* and 'the Silence from Järvenpää' became as much of a talking point as the music. Continually pestered about an Eighth Symphony, the composer battled alcohol addiction, depression and above all self-criticism; it is generally thought that the completed symphony was burnt in the fireplace at Ainola. The figure at the centre of this poem is based on the historical Jean Sibelius, imagined late in life when past and present are less distinct. But he is also (to use T.S.Eliot's phrase) a 'compound ghost', the representative of any artist who is struggling to create.

Acknowledgements

Poems have appeared in the following publications and thanks are due to the editors:

Acumen ('Rite', extract from 'The Silence')
Agenda (extract from 'The Silence')
The Bow-Wow Shop ('Nebamun's Tomb')
The High Window (extract from 'The Silence')
The Hudson Review ('To a Lost Friend', 'After Hölderlin: Homecoming')
Ink Sweat & Tears ('Totem')
London Magazine ('Sibelius', 'On St Cecilia's Day', 'Woden', 'Buzzard', 'Under')
Magma ('Five Hilliard Miniatures')
Manhattan Review ('Airmail for Chief Seattle', extract from 'The Silence')
PN Review (Three poems from 'Heath', 'Flight Path', 'From the Peak')
POEM ('Evensong')
Poetry Ireland Review ('After Hölderlin: Hyperion's Song of Destiny')
The Reader (extract from 'The Silence')
A Room to Live In (Salt) ('Stray Objects')
Salamander ('Clearing')
The Spectator ('Kew', 'Two Roads', 'X5', 'Praise for', 'Compleat')
Stand Magazine ('Chalk', extract from 'The Silence')
The Times Literary Supplement ('Bunker', '1d', 'Tree Rings')
The Tree Line (Worple Press, 2017) ('Tree Rings')
The Warwick Review ('Visionary')
Wild Court ('Fontevraud', extract from 'The Silence')

The 'Heath' poems and 'Flight Path' are from a collaboration with Penelope Shuttle, *Heath*, published by Nine Arches Press (2016).

'Nebamun's Tomb' appeared as a pamphlet from Rack Press in 2016.

The epigraph to this collection is taken from the last line of 'Clearances' by Seamus Heaney, *The Haw Lantern* (Faber, 1987).

The lines quoted at the start of 'The Silence' are from 'Little Gidding' by T.S. Eliot, *Collected Poems, 1909–1962* (Faber, 2017).

With thanks to the Society of Authors for an Authors' Foundation Award in 2015 to help with the writing of 'The Silence' and to the trustees of Hawthornden Writers' Retreat for residencies in 2010 and 2017 during which some of these poems were composed.